Burlesque Baking

Burlesque Baking

The art of show-stopping, decadent cakes

Charlotte White

Photography by
Clare Winfield

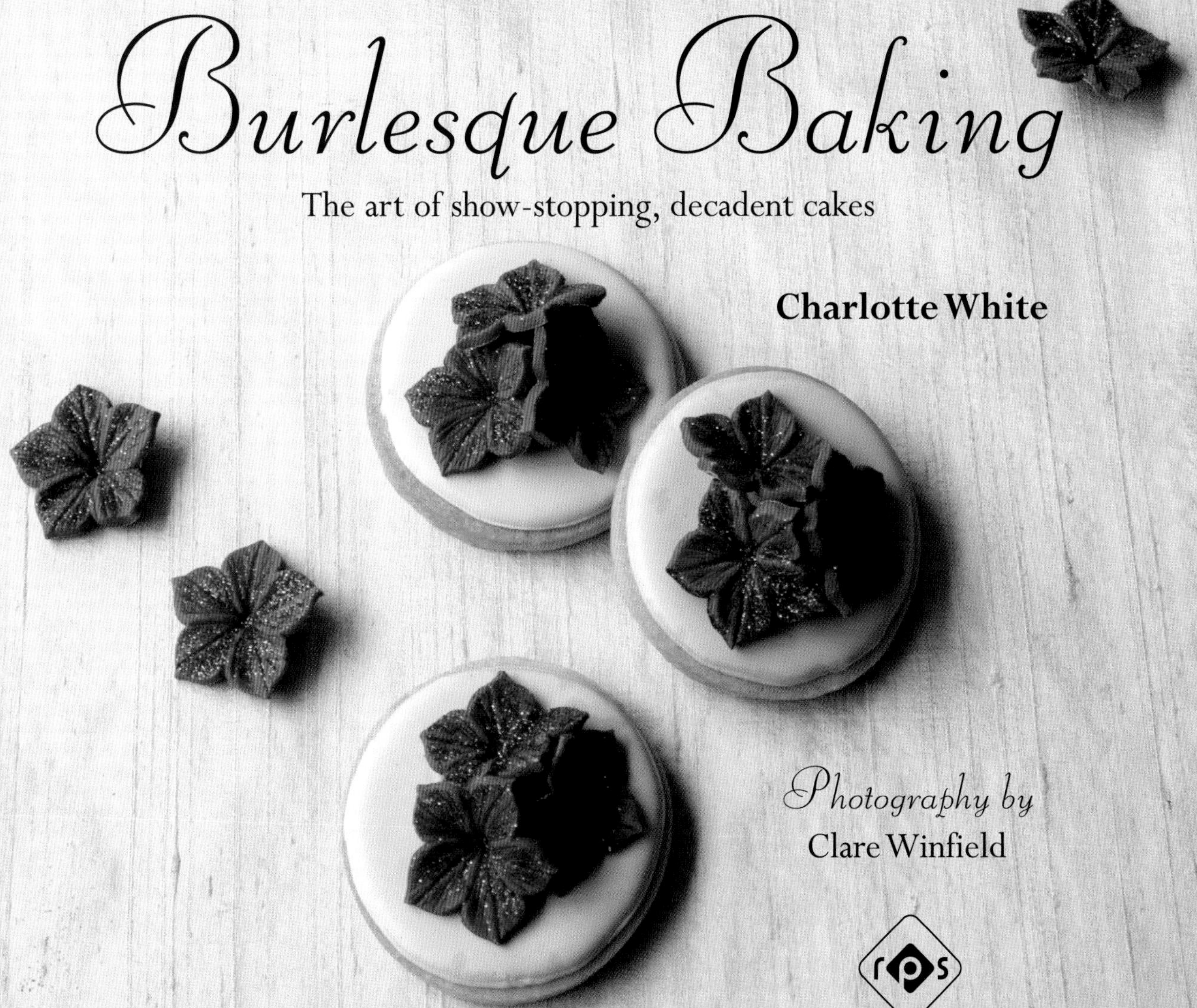

RYLAND PETERS & SMALL
LONDON • NEW YORK

Text © Charlotte White 2014
Design and photographs © Ryland Peters & Small 2014

ISBN: 978-1-84975-496-5

A CIP record for this book is available from
the British Library.

US Library of Congress cataloging-in-Publication Data has
been applied for.

Printed in China.

Acknowledgments

This book is dedicated to all of the incredible, beautiful women who
have inspired my work, with thanks to the artists who have inspired
these projects, to my mother for her constant encouragement, to
my nana for getting me hooked on baking, and to Nigella Lawson
for her invaluable advice. Special thanks to the incomparable
Catherine D'Lish for her words and support. Thank you to Rebecca
Woods for making an introduction that made a dream come true
and to everyone at RPS who has worked so hard to make this dream
a reality, especially Nathan Joyce. Thank you to Leslie, Barbara,
Clare and Lisa for your creativity and for helping me create the
anti-twee! Thank you to Lisa-Jane Brown for taking my picture,
to Revival Retro for the beautiful frock and to Elbie Van Eeden
for making me look pretty in it! Thanks also to Andrew at
Café de Paris. Thank you to Sophie and Alice at Holloway Smith
Noir (www.hollowaysmithnoir.com) for the beautiful teasewear,
Oliver McAllister at KitchenAid (www.kitchenaid.com),
Lisa Slatter at Knightsbridge PME (www.cakedecoration.co.uk),
Renshaw (www.renshawbaking.com), Louisa Russell at Blossom
Sugarart (www.blossomsugarart.net), and Janet Sawyer at LittlePod
Vanilla (www.littlepod.co.uk). Thank you to Tim Reed for all of
your help. Thank you to my family and urban family for your
unending love and support. To my wonderful husband, Chris,
without whom none of this would be possible – you are fabulous.

DESIGN Barbara Zuñiga
EDITORS Rebecca Woods and Nathan Joyce
HEAD OF PRODUCTION Patricia Harrington
ART DIRECTOR Leslie Harrington
EDITORIAL DIRECTOR Julia Charles
INDEXER Hilary Bird

First published in 2014 by **Ryland Peters & Small**
20–21 Jockey's Fields, London WC1R 4BW
and
519 Broadway, 5th Floor, New York, NY 10012
www.rylandpeters.com
10 9 8 7 6 5 4 3 2 1

Notes

– Eggs used in this book are UK large and
US extra large.
– The author uses particular brands of Sugarflair
and PME food colouring pastes, so colour
descriptions refer to these shades; if you choose
alternative brands, we suggest that you use the
photographs in this book to match the colour.
– Most of the cake supplies used in this book can
be found through www.globalsugarart.com,
www.wilton.com, www.cakedecoration.co.uk
and www.cakecraftworld.co.uk.

Contents

Preface

Sean McCall

Charlotte White states that she believes in 'beauty, love, and delicious cake.' As a Burlesque performer, costumer, teacher and 'sexpert', I believe in beauty, love and the deliciousness of women. The very best Burlesque performers understand the appeal of presenting a visual feast, adorning themselves in lavish garments that glorify the luscious woman wrapped inside. As entertainers, they know that elaborate and glamorous garb creates an air of excitement upon first viewing. The woman is 'gilded' and although she may also be shrouded in an air of mystique, the spectator knows that she will soon disrobe, and they'll be privy to what lies underneath… they'll possibly fantasize about her smooth flesh, her feminine curves…

This experience is not unlike what goes through one's mind when first seeing a sumptuous cake. The more beautiful and spectacular the presentation, the more one imagines how moist and delicious the cake inside will be. However, most will find that dream as they may, their experience with the cake will be far more intimate than their encounters with their favourite entertainers!

The best costumes worn by the premier Burlesque artists today are spectacular displays of excessiveness. There is nothing practical or modest about them. These women delight in displays of extravagance and elegance that are nothing but pure indulgence of their wildest fantasies. The costuming is meant to stimulate the imagination and inspire, to tease and titillate, to attract the eye and envy. Contemporary cake decoration has evolved in a similar way to the advancement of Burlesque costuming. Although many are based on classic designs, there is a decadence in both arts that has developed over the years; today's masterpieces are wonders to behold.

D'Lish

www.catherinedlish.com

Lisa Jane Photography

Welcome to the show...

Burlesque performers have a rule of thumb; that if an item of clothing cannot be seen from the back of the audience, it just isn't worth wearing. We are talking rhinestones, sequins, glittering sparkling jewels and all things that entice and delight the eye. I believe that this very same principle should apply to cakes and all tasty treats.

Given that we eat with our eyes before we devour with our mouths, it is the duty of each and every cake, cupcake and cookie to be decorated. In the pages of this book, I will share with you my very favourite recipes for truly delicious bakes but also hope to inspire you to dress them up in such a way that they will attract little gasps of excitement from across a crowded room.

What better way to achieve this reaction than to look to the world of Burlesque for inspiration? The designs that I have created for this book have each taken a spectacular Burlesque performer as its muse – her costume, her performance, her legacy, her name – each facet reflected in icing.

Each individual cake and bake is conceived of a desire to enchant and to give pleasure. Sometimes it holds the spotlight in pride of place, posing for photographs. Sometimes it hides in a box ready for the big reveal, heralded by candles and singing. Cakes generally know how to make an entrance that awakens our excitement and anticipation.

So, welcome to Burlesque Baking. Welcome to the show!

Charlotte
x

www.restorationcake.co.uk

Glossary of Terms & Essential Advice

Blossom/Flower Cutters: The best flower cutters come with individual veining moulds to match each cutter. These moulds add realistic details to the flowers and are easy to use.

Cake Pans: The recipes in this book will all make enough batter for one standard 20-cm/8-inch sandwich tin/round cake pan (or one batch of 12 cupcakes or 16 mini cakes – see below). You will need to double the quantity to make the 2 layers of cake required for one of the larger cakes. Remember to line the base of your cake pans with parchment paper.

Chocolate Cigarellos: Available online, but always order more than you need to allow for any breakages in transit.

Cookie Cutters: I have used a 5-cm/2-inch round and 5-cm/2-inch heart cookie cutters. If you use a smaller cutter, you will need to reduce your baking time.

Cornflour/Cornstarch: I find cornflour/cornstarch the best for preventing my sugarpaste from sticking when rolling out. You can use icing/confectioners' sugar as an alternative.

Cupcakes: Each recipe will make 12 cupcakes.

Glitters: Keep a selection of edible glitters in your kit and remember that white glitter goes with everything!

Lustres and Dust Colours: Used as dust to add extra detail to sugar flowers, these can also be mixed with clear alcohol (usually vodka) to create an edible paint.

Marzipan Spacers: Used as a guide to roll out sugarpaste and cookie dough to a uniform thickness.

Metallic Food Paint: Use to add shimmer and shine!

Mini Cakes: I bake my mini cakes using a special mini-cake tin, which has 16 small cavities designed to bake 5-cm/2-inch mini cakes to perfection. You can achieve the same effect by cutting small rounds out of a larger cake using a cookie cutter, but you will make fewer cakes doing it this way.

Paste (or Gel) Colours: To add colour to sugarpaste and royal icing, you will need to use concentrated paste colours (avoid liquid colours as these lead to sticky sugarpaste and runny royal icing). Add your colour by dipping a cocktail stick/toothpick into the paste and then wiping this into your sugarpaste or dipping into your royal icing.

Piping Bags: Parchment piping bags are the best, cheapest and most convenient.

Piping Nozzles: You will only need a few nozzles for these projects; a fine round nozzle used for small pearls and dots, a medium round nozzle for larger pearls and a medium leaf nozzle to create ruffles. A small leaf nozzle, for adding finishing flourishes, is also really useful.

Pizza Wheel: Use a pizza wheel to cut your sugarpaste as the circular blade does not cause dragging like a knife will.

Rolling Pin: You will need a good non-stick rolling pin to work with sugarpaste. I recommend using a 40-cm/16-inch rolling pin for covering cakes and a 15-cm/6-inch rolling pin for making small decorations.

Royal Icing: A mixture of egg albumen and icing sugar which has a glossy elasticity when piped and dries hard. I always use the ready-mixed packets of Royal Icing Sugar that only require water and a thorough mixing. I recommend using a freestanding mixer for this.

Side Scraper: Used to create a perfect buttercream finish on cakes.

Straight-edged Smoother: Used to create a perfectly smooth finish on sugarpaste covered cakes. Like a little plastic iron!

Sugarpaste: Is also known as fondant icing and ready-to-roll icing.

Tylose Powder/CMC: A special powder that can be kneaded into sugarpaste allowing it to dry hard, which is essential for creating sugar flowers.

Vanilla Extract/Pods: Use the best vanilla that you can afford!

Classic Victoria Sponge Cake

This recipe has been adapted from a recipe featured in *The Book of Good Housekeeping*, originally published in 1944. Why mess with a classic? These basic proportions result in a deliciously light and fluffy sponge. You will need to amend your ingredient quantities for large and small bakes but I have done this for you, because I'm nice like that.

FOR 1 LARGE CAKE:

340 g / 2 sticks plus 6 tablespoons unsalted butter

340 g / 1⅔ cups caster / granulated sugar

6 large eggs

2 teaspoons vanilla extract

340 g / 2⅔ cups self-raising / self-rising flour

1½ teaspoons baking powder

6 tablespoons whole milk

FOR 12 CUPCAKES OR 16 MINI CAKES:

170 g / 1 stick plus 3 tablespoons unsalted butter

170 g / ¾ cup plus 1 tablespoon caster / granulated sugar

3 large eggs

1 teaspoon vanilla extract

170 g / 1⅓ cups self-raising / self-rising flour

¾ teaspoon baking powder

3 tablespoons whole milk

EQUIPMENT:

a 12-hole cupcake pan,

a 16-hole mini cake pan, or

2 x 20-cm / 8-inch cake pans

1 Preheat your oven to 180°C (350°F) Gas 4.

2 Cream together the butter and sugar until they are pale and creamy. Never underestimate the time that it will take to complete this step – allow a good 5 minutes in a freestanding mixer (or with an electric hand whisk) and do not rush.

3 Add one egg at a time, allowing each egg to be fully incorporated before adding the next (this patience should prevent curdling), then add the vanilla.

4 Sift the flour and baking powder into a separate bowl and fold into your wet ingredients with a large spoon. Be gentle and stop mixing as soon as the flour is incorporated. Add enough milk to make a dropping consistency – the cake mixture should dollop off of your wooden spoon like thick cream. You may not need to add the full amount of milk listed here.

5 Divide the mixture between the 12 cupcake cases, the 16 holes of the mini-cake pan or the 2 prepared sandwich tins / round cake pans and bake in the preheated oven. Give the cupcakes and mini cakes about 20 minutes and the larger cakes 35–40 minutes, or until the cakes are risen and a skewer inserted into the cake comes out clean. Allow them to cool in their pans for 5 minutes before turning out onto a wire rack to cool completely.

Variation

To make a large Lemon Victoria Sponge, replace your vanilla extract with the zest of 2 lemons and the juice of one lemon. Warm the juice of your second lemon with 50 g / ¼ cup caster / granulated sugar to create a syrup, which can be drizzled over the hot cakes as soon as they come out of the oven. (You could make lemon cupcakes or mini cakes too, simply halving the quantities of lemon and sugar.)

Chocolate Mud Cake

I learned this recipe many years ago from my first cake teacher. The mixture is more like a liquid batter that needs to be poured into your cake pans. Trust me, this mix rises beautifully and the cake keeps really well… if you can bear to keep it!

220 g / 7½ oz. dark
chocolate

220 g / 2 sticks less 1
tablespoon unsalted butter

2 tablespoons instant coffee
granules

160 ml / ¾ cup water

125 g / 1 cup plain / all-
purpose flour

125 g / 1 cup self-
raising / self-rising flour

40 g / ⅓ cup cocoa powder

½ teaspoon bicarbonate
of soda / baking soda

480 g / 2 ½ cups caster /
granulated sugar

a pinch of salt

4 large eggs

2½ tablespoons vegetable oil

110 ml / a scant ½ cup
buttermilk

EQUIPMENT:

2 x 20-cm / 8-inch sandwich
tins / round cake pans, lined
and greased

Makes 1 large cake, 24
cupcakes or 32 mini cakes

1 Preheat your oven to 160°C (325°F) Gas 3.

2 Melt the chocolate and the butter in a small saucepan with the instant coffee granules and 160 ml / ⅔ cup water. Keep the temperature low and stir the mixture occasionally; turn off the heat when only a few small lumps of chocolate remain – these will melt in the heat of the mixture and turning the heat off early prevents burning.

3 Sift the flours, cocoa powder, bicarbonate of soda / baking soda and sugar into a bowl and add the salt. Make a small well in the centre and set aside.

4 Beat the eggs, oil and buttermilk together in a jug / pitcher before tipping this mixture into the dry ingredients and stirring it into a thick paste.

5 Pour the melted chocolate and butter mixture on top of this paste and fold everything together with a wooden spoon until you have one glossy mixture in the bowl.

6 Divide your cake mixture between two prepared cake pans and bake in the preheated oven for about 40 minutes or until a skewer comes out clean (or with only a few tiny crumbs attached to it). Allow the cakes to cool completely in their pans.

Salted Caramel Cake

Everyone goes crazy for salted caramel and this dangerously moreish cake has a taste of caramel running right the way through every mouthful.

For the Caramel Syrup:

225 g/1 cup plus 2 tablespoons caster/granulated sugar

250 ml/1 cup boiling water

For the Caramel Cake:

225 g/2 sticks less 1 tablespoon unsalted butter

380 g/2 cups less 2 tablespoons caster/granulated sugar

4 large eggs

480 g/3 ¾ cups plain/all-purpose flour

1 tablespoon baking powder

½ teaspoon salt

250 ml/1 cup whole milk

2 teaspoons caramel essence or 1 teaspoon vanilla extract

Equipment:

2 x 20-cm/8-inch sandwich tins/round cake pans, lined and greased

Makes 1 large cake, 24 cupcakes or 32 mini cakes

1 To make the caramel syrup, heat the sugar in a heavy-bottomed saucepan until it goes brown and treacly, a little darker than golden syrup/light corn syrup, with no lumps. Stir it every now and then but do not leave the room while the sugar is heating as it will go from nicely caramelized to burnt very quickly!

2 Add the boiling water very carefully as the pan will spit. Try pouring the water down the side of the saucepan and wear an oven glove/mitt if you are worried. Stir the water into the syrup for 1 minute until they have completely combined, then remove the pan from the heat and allow the syrup to cool. You can make the syrup a day or two in advance if you like and store in an airtight container until needed.

3 To make the caramel cake, preheat your oven to 180°C (350°F) Gas 4. Cream together the butter and the sugar until you have a pale and creamy mixture. This should take around 5 minutes in a freestanding mixer (or with a hand-held electric mixer). Allowing time to mix thoroughly will set you up for a wonderfully light cake.

4 Add the eggs, one at a time, making sure that each egg is fully incorporated before adding the next, then add 125 ml/½ cup of your caramel syrup to the mixture and beat briefly until smooth and golden. You will need the remaining syrup for your Salted Caramel Buttercream (see page 13).

5 Sift your flour, baking powder and salt into another bowl and combine your milk and caramel essence in a jug/pitcher. Fold one third of your dry ingredients into the cake mixture followed by one half of your milk and essence. Add another third of your dry ingredients, followed by your remaining milk. Remember to stir well after each addition to ensure that all ingredients are incorporated. Finish off with the final third of your dry ingredients.

6 Divide your cake mixture between two prepared cake pans and bake in the preheated oven for 35–45 minutes. The cake is done when it has risen beautifully and a cake tester comes out clean. Leave the cakes to cool in their pans for 5 minutes before turning out onto a wire rack to cool completely.

Classic Cookies

I like to think of this recipe as going back to a time when ingredients were measured proportionally – half fat, half sugar, then an equal amount of flour and an egg and you're good to go!

200 g/1 stick plus 5
  tablespoons unsalted
  butter

200 g/1 cup golden
  caster/raw cane or regular
  granulated sugar

1 large egg

choice of flavourings:
  for vanilla cookies add the
  seeds from 1 vanilla bean;
  for chocolate cookies add
  50 g/6 tablespoons cocoa
  powder; for lemon cookies
  add the grated zest of 1
  lemon

400 g/3 cups plus 2
  tablespoons plain/all-
  purpose flour (reduce this
  amount by 50 g/6
  tablespoons if making
  chocolate cookies), plus
  extra for dusting

EQUIPMENT:

a non-stick rolling pin

marzipan spacers

a 5-cm/2-inch (round or
  heart-shaped) cookie
  cutter

a baking sheet lined with
  baking parchment

Makes 12 cookies

1 Begin by creaming together the butter and sugar in a freestanding mixer. Allow for 3 minutes of beating to ensure that they are fully combined. You can do this by hand but be prepared for a workout.

2 Add the egg and beat until incorporated, then add your desired flavouring and beat in.

3 Add the flour and beat until the mixture forms a ball of dough. Remove the dough from your mixer and wrap tightly in clingfilm/plastic wrap. This will need to chill in the fridge for at least 30 minutes before you use it and you will need the dough to be cold as you roll it out. You can make your dough up to 1 week in advance.

4 When you are ready to bake your cookies, preheat your oven to 180°C (350°F) Gas 4.

5 Roll out your dough on a floured surface, using marzipan spacers placed on either side of the dough to give you an even thickness. Don't be tempted to knead your dough to warm it up – you will need to work hard to flatten it, but the dough needs to be cold for the cookies to hold their shape.

6 Cut out 12 cookies using the cookie cutter and lay these on the baking sheet. Put the baking sheet in the fridge for 10 minutes to chill the cookies before baking.

7 These cookies will take around 10 minutes to bake in the preheated oven and are ready when they are golden brown and firm. Allow them to cool completely on a wire rack before storing in an airtight container. You can store them for up to 2 weeks, if you can resist them!

Buttercream

All buttercreams begin in the same way. I have added a few basic flavour variations to allow you to use your buttercream to complement your cake. I like to beat my buttercream for a good 5 minutes to really fuse the sugar and butter together so that the end result is light, smooth and deliciously creamy.

250 g / 2 sticks unsalted butter, softened

choice of flavourings:
  for vanilla buttercream add 2 teaspoons vanilla extract or the seeds from 1 vanilla bean;
  for chocolate buttercream add 50 g / 6 tablespoons cocoa powder;
  for lemon buttercream add 2 tablespoons prepared lemon curd; for salted caramel buttercream add 125 ml / ½ cup caramel syrup (see page 11) and ½ teaspoon fine table salt

350 g / 3¼ cups icing / confectioners' sugar

Makes sufficient buttercream for 1 large cake, 24 cupcakes or 32 mini cakes

1 Roughly carve up the butter and beat in a freestanding mixer for 3 minutes until creamy. You can also do this by hand or using a hand-held electric mixer and a large mixing bowl, although you may find that this takes longer.

2 Add your desired flavouring and beat in.

3 Once your flavour is fully incorporated, add 250 g / 2⅓ cups of the icing / confectioners' sugar and beat for 1 minute. Check the consistency of your buttercream – you are aiming for the thickness of thick whipped cream – if your buttercream is too runny, add the remaining icing / confectioners' sugar. You will then need to beat the buttercream for a further 5 minutes, until the sugar is completely incorporated.

The Art of Covering Up

A valuable talent for any Burlesque beauty.

a 20-cm/8-inch cake
(see pages 9–11, although
Victoria Sponge is easiest
for beginners)
OR 16 Mini Cakes
(see page 9)

1 quantity Buttercream
(see page 13)

jam in a flavour of your
choice (optional)

750 g/26 oz. sugarpaste
(refer to the relevant
recipe for colour)

food colouring paste (refer to
the relevant recipe for
colour)

cornflour/cornstarch,
for dusting

EQUIPMENT:

a large serrated knife

a large palette knife

a side scraper

a large non-stick rolling pin

a straight-edge smoother

marzipan spacers

a pizza wheel

ribbon (refer to the relevant
recipe for colour)

1 *Large cakes*: To cover a large cake, you will need to begin by levelling off your 2 cakes. Cakes rarely come out of the oven perfectly level so you will need to remove the peaks. Take your two cakes, still in their cake pans, lay a serrated knife across the top of your cake pan and, using this as a guide, carefully cut away any cake that has risen above the pan. Remove your cakes from their pans. Spread the cut side of one cake with jam (if desired) and the cut side of the other cake with buttercream. Sandwich these two halves of cake together so that the jam and buttercream are in the middle of the finished cake. This leaves us with a perfectly flat top to cover with sugarpaste.

Small cakes: If you are covering mini cakes, begin by running a sharp knife across the top edge of the cake pan, using this as a guide to remove any risen tops while the cakes are still in the pan. When you pop your mini cakes out, the cut edges should become your bottom edge so that the top edge is perfectly flat. As these cakes are so small, you will not need to fill the middle with buttercream, instead proceed to step 2.

2 Use your (remaining) buttercream to cover the top and sides of your cake. This is best done with a large palette knife. Start by spreading buttercream on the top and then the sides of the cake.

3 To tidy the edges, hold the side scraper tool flush against your work surface and then press the flat panel lightly into the buttercream on the side of your cake. Then pull the scraper slowly around the cake to create an even surface. Finish off by scraping the top edges of the cake in towards the centre to achieve a clean top edge. This buttercream is used to keep the cake moist and to create an adhesive for the sugarpaste – so do not be too generous! Set your prepared cake aside and clean your work surface.

4 Rub a small amount of cornflour/cornstarch onto your hands and knead your sugarpaste for 3–5 minutes on a clean work surface. Kneading causes the sugarpaste to warm up, which results in a much smoother finish.

5 To add colour to your sugarpaste, dip a cocktail stick/toothpick into the colouring paste and then dip the colour into your sugarpaste. You can always add more colour to create a stronger shade, but it is trickier to take it away if you want it to be more subtle. If you want a strong colour such as jet black or scarlet red, you will need to buy pre-coloured sugarpaste.

6 Once you are happy that your sugarpaste feels sufficiently smooth and pliable under your hands and there are no streaks of colour, dust a small amount of cornflour/cornstarch onto your work surface and place your ball of sugarpaste on top. Press the sugarpaste down into a chunky flat disc.

7 Lay your marzipan spacers either side of your sugarpaste and begin rolling it out in long fluid strokes. If you roll once forwards and once back, before lifting and turning the sugarpaste by a quarter turn and repeating this process, you should end up with a nice even roll and something resembling a circle of sugarpaste. You will know that you have finished rolling out when your rolling pin rests on the top of the guiding marzipan spacers.

8 Slide your hands underneath the sugarpaste, keeping your fingers together so that they do not poke through, until they are in the centre of the circle. Gently lift the sugarpaste and hold it above your cake. Line up your hands with the centre of the cake and carefully lower the sugarpaste onto it.

9 Using the flat of your hand, gently press onto the top edges of the cake to secure the sugarpaste. Use a gentle stroking motion to secure the sugarpaste to the sides of your cake, always smoothing upwards to prevent pulling on the sugarpaste and causing any breakage.

10 Once you have smoothed the sides of your cake all the way down to the work surface, trim away any excess sugarpaste with a pizza wheel.

11 Use your straight-edge smoother to create a really polished finish on your cake. With the straight-edge flush against the work surface, and the flat panel pressed lightly on the sides of your cake, run the smoother around the sides to iron out any rough surfaces. Go around the cake 3–4 times and then give the top a final polish with your smoother. If you find any air bubbles, these can be popped with a cocktail stick/toothpick and smoothed out.

12 Finish the bottom edge of your cake with a ribbon, secured with a dab of royal icing or a little sticky tape (the tape should only touch the ribbon itself and not the cake).

THE GAIETY THEATRE

I can think of nowhere more fabulous to begin!

Miss Cherry Shakewell Cake

a 20-cm / 8-inch Chocolate
Mud Cake (see page 10)

150 g / ½ cup black cherry
preserve

1 quantity Chocolate
Buttercream (see page 13)

1 quantity Vanilla
Buttercream (see page 13)

about 80 white chocolate
cigarellos

400 g / 14 oz. fresh cherries

hologram red edible glitter

EQUIPMENT:

a large serrated knife

a large palette knife

a side scraper

red organza ribbon

Serves up to 20

Inspired by the Lady of the Cake, Cherry Shakewell, this cake is gorgeous, crowned with glittering cherries. I have used vanilla buttercream and white chocolate cigarellos on the outside to conceal the deep dark chocolate and black cherries within.

1 Begin by preparing your cake in much the same way as we did in The Art of Covering Up (see page 14), removing any peaks from your cakes, then removing them from their pans.

2 Spread the cut side of one cake with black cherry preserve and the cut side of the other cake with the Chocolate Buttercream. Sandwich your cakes together so that the preserve and buttercream are in the centre.

3 Dollop a friendly helping of Vanilla Buttercream onto the top of your cake and, using a large palette knife, spread the buttercream over the top and sides of the cake. Tidy up the edges of your cake by holding the side scraper flush against your work surface and slightly into the buttercream on the side of your cake. Slowly, pull the scraper towards you and you should see the excess buttercream being removed as you work around the cake. You will need to stop and clean off the scraper every now and then to create a smooth finish. Use your scraper to scrape the top edges of the cake in towards the centre to achieve a clean top edge (see page 14).

4 Line up your chocolate cigarellos around the edge of your cake, one by one, pressing each cigarello lightly into the buttercream to secure. When you have completely covered the outside of your cake, carefully tie a ribbon around the middle of the cake; this makes the cake look pretty and also helps to keep the cigarellos secure.

5 Rinse your cherries under cold water, then pat dry with paper towels. Whilst still on the towel, take a hearty pinch of the red edible glitter and sprinkle this onto your cherries. Once you are content that they are sufficiently glistening, arrange them atop your cake like precious jewels.

Miss Lady Alex Cookies

12 Classic Cookies
(see page 12)

500 g / 1 lb. 2 oz. black
sugarpaste

125 g / 1 cup royal icing

teal food colouring paste

violet food colouring paste

Equipment:

3 parchment piping bags
fitted with fine round
nozzles/tips

a cocktail stick/toothpick

a paintbrush

Makes 12

This cookie takes no prisoners and demands your full attention, like her fabulous hostess namesake!

1 Begin by covering your cookies with sugarpaste. To add drama to my cookies, I have used pre-coloured black sugarpaste. If you want to use a dark colour, you will need to buy your paste pre-coloured.

2 Mix up your royal icing according to the packet instructions. Divide the royal icing into three and colour one portion in teal, one portion violet and leave the third portion white. Fill one piping bag one-quarter full with teal royal icing, fill the second with the same amount of violet royal icing and the third with the same amount of white royal icing. Your piping bag should be closed so tightly that you only have to squeeze very gently to make the icing come out of the nozzle/tip.

3 Use a cocktail stick/toothpick to score a light swirl line into your sugarpaste from just short of one side of your cookie to the opposite side. Pipe tiny dots of your teal royal icing along this line, flattening any points in the icing with a paintbrush. Hold your piping nozzle/tip just above the sugarpaste and squeeze gently until you are happy with the size of your dot.

4 Pipe a line of white royal icing dots on either side of your teal line. Stop your line of white dots just short of the end of your teal dots as we want to create a pointed end to the curved line, with the final teal dot as the point.

5 Repeat this process by piping a line of violet dots on either side of your white line. Again, stop your line of violet dots just short of the end of your white dots. You should have a pronounced point at the end of your swirl now.

6 Start another two swirl lines either side of the swirl that you have created, beginning again by scoring a guideline using a cocktail stick/toothpick. Leave the royal icing to dry and then they're ready to serve!

Miss Dixie Evans Mini Cakes

16 x 5-cm / 2-inch Mini
 Cakes (see page 9)

½ quantity Buttercream
 (see page 13)

500 g / 1 lb. 2 oz. white
 sugarpaste

cornflour / cornstarch,
 for dusting

250 g / 2¼ cups royal icing
 sugar

pearlescent white metallic
 food paint or pearl lustre
 (I favour pearlescent white
 metallic food paint for
 this job, but any pearl
 lustre mixed with a little
 clear alcohol, such as
 vodka, will work)

EQUIPMENT:

16 x 16-cm / 6½ inch lengths
 of thin silver ribbon

a parchment piping bag
 fitted with a fine round
 nozzle / tip

a paintbrush

(see also equipment required
 for covering a cake on
 page 14)

Makes 16

Shimmering pearls may be this sensational girl's best friend. Inspired by the incomparable Miss Dixie Evans — she's hotter than a hydrogen bomb and always as sweet as sugar.

1 Begin by covering your mini cakes in buttercream and then sugarpaste, using the same technique detailed in The Art of Covering Up on pages 14–15. You may find this a little fiddly at first as smaller cakes require more nimble fingers than larger ones!

2 Mix up your royal icing according to the packet instructions, and fill your piping bag one-quarter full. Close up the open end of your piping bag and ensure that the icing is all squeezed down towards the piping nozzle / tip. Your piping bag should be closed so tightly that you only have to squeeze very gently to make the icing come out of the nozzle / tip.

3 Wrap a length of silver ribbon around each cake, securing with a small dot of royal icing from your piping bag.

4 To pipe a pearl, point your piping bag straight at the cake, with the nozzle / tip very close to but not quite touching the surface. Gently squeeze your piping bag until you are happy with the size of the pearl on the cake — the longer you squeeze, the larger the pearl you will create. When you are happy, stop squeezing the piping bag and pull the nozzle away from the cake. If your pearl has a slight peak, this can be dampened down with a paintbrush. Repeat this process until your cake is completely covered with pearls and leave these to dry for at least 30 minutes.

5 Once the pearls are dry, use the paintbrush to paint each one with the food paint or lustre to make them shine.

Miss Anna Fur Laxis Cupcakes

½ quantity Buttercream
(see page 13)

12 Cupcakes (see page 9)

500 g / 1 lb. 2 oz. white
sugarpaste

hot pink food colouring
paste

cornflour / cornstarch,
for dusting

250 g / 2¼ cups royal icing
sugar

EQUIPMENT:

marzipan spacers

a round cookie cutter the
same size as the top of
your cupcake

a parchment piping bag
fitted with a medium
round nozzle / tip

a paintbrush

Makes 12

Pretty – but also pretty deadly – in polka dots, these
cupcakes, inspired by the wonderful Anna Fur Laxis,
are guaranteed to impress.

1 Begin by spreading a thin layer of buttercream over the top of each cupcake,
which will serve not only to keep your cupcake moist but will act as a
delicious adhesive for your sugarpaste covering.

2 Knead your sugarpaste until smooth, then colour it to a hot pink using the
paste colour, added a little at a time with a cocktail stick/toothpick. On a
surface lightly dusted with cornflour/cornstarch, roll out the pink sugarpaste with
a non-stick rolling pin, using marzipan spacers as a guide for the even thickness of
your icing. Cut out 12 circles of sugarpaste using the cookie cutter.

3 Take a cupcake and lay a circle of sugarpaste on top, pressing down lightly
with your palm. Once the sugarpaste has adhered, cup your hand and use
this in a slow twisting motion as a rounded smoother to smooth the sugarpaste onto
your cupcake. The warmth of your palm will create a beautifully smooth finish.

4 Mix up your royal icing according to the packet instructions, and fill your
piping bag one-quarter full. Close up the open end of your piping bag and
ensure that the icing is all squeezed down towards the piping nozzle/tip. Your
piping bag should be closed so tightly that you only have to squeeze very gently
to make the icing come out of the nozzle/tip.

5 To pipe a pearl, point your piping bag straight at the cake, with the
nozzle/tip very close to but not quite touching the surface. Gently squeeze
your piping bag until you are happy with the size of the pearl on the cake – the
longer you squeeze, the larger the pearl you will create. When you are happy, stop
squeezing the piping bag and pull the nozzle away from the cake. If your pearl has
a slight peak, this can be dampened down with a paintbrush. I think that the pearls
look most effective arranged into little lines of polka dots. Repeat to decorate
all of your cupcakes then leave the icing to set.

Miss Strawberry Siren Cake

a 20-cm/8-inch Cake in
   any flavour you wish
   (see pages 9–11)

1 quantity Buttercream
   (see page 13)

1 kg/2¼ lbs. white sugarpaste

spruce green food colouring paste

cornflour/cornstarch,
   for dusting

125 g/1 cup royal icing sugar

hologram white edible glitter

FOR THE SUGAR FLOWERS:

2 teaspoons tylose powder

500 g/1 lb. 2 oz. white
   sugarpaste

hot pink and violet food
   colouring pastes

aubergine and burgundy dust
   food colours

clear alcohol, such as vodka
   (optional)

EQUIPMENT:

green ribbon

a selection of flower cutters and
   moulds (I have used blossom,
   hydrangea, cherry blossom
   and petunia)

a paintbrush

(see also equipment required for
   covering a cake on page 14)

Serves up to 20

Inspired by the precious petal of Burlesque, Strawberry Siren, this cake looks fabulous in cascading florals.

1 Begin by dyeing the 1 kg/2¼ lbs. sugarpaste spruce green. Cover your cake in buttercream and then the sugarpaste, using the same technique as we used in The Art of Covering Up on pages 14–15, finishing with a green ribbon.

2 For the exotic flowers that will adorn the cake, knead the tylose powder into the sugarpaste until the powder has completely disappeared into the paste. Divide this flower-making paste into three portions and colour one hot pink and one violet, leaving the final portion of sugarpaste white. Wrap any sugarpaste that you are not using in clingfilm/plastic wrap to prevent it from drying out.

3 One colour at a time, roll out your paste until it is around 2 mm/1⁄16 inch thick. Use your cutters to cut out flower shapes from the sugarpaste.

4 While the sugar flowers are still soft, lay them one by one into a veining mould that has been lightly dusted with cornflour/cornstarch. Close the mould and give the outside a little squeeze; when you open it, you should find that the flower is now beautifully detailed. Repeat with the remaining 2 sugarpaste colours and set these flowers aside to dry for at least an hour. You can make flowers days in advance and keep them in a cardboard box.

5 Add more colour and depth to your flowers by brushing them with dust colours. Alternatively, mix the dusts with clear alcohol to make an edible paint.

6 Mix up your royal icing according to the packet instructions. To stick your flowers to the cake, take a little icing on a small palette knife and spread onto the back of each flower. You should only need a small amount of icing to make the flowers stick. Start building up your flowers from the bottom of the cake, so that the higher flowers are supported by the lower ones. Mix up your colours and flower types to create a truly unique finish.

7 Sprinkle your glitter liberally over the cake from a height to create an even coating and make it sparkle and shine!

MINSKY'S BURLESQUE THEATRE

By now you should be finding your feet, learning to thrill the crowd with your bakes

Miss Scarlet Delights Cookies

12 Classic Cookies
(see page 12)

500 g/1 lb. 2 oz. sugarpaste

cornflour/cornstarch,
for dusting

250 g/2 cups royal icing
sugar

red extra food colouring
paste

EQUIPMENT:

marzipan spacers

the same cookie cutter you
used to make the cookies

a paintbrush

a parchment piping bag
fitted with a small leaf
piping nozzle/tip

Makes 12

Like their namesake, the delightful Scarlet Delights, these cookies are sweet and moreish! A vision in vermillion.

1 Begin by covering your cookies with sugarpaste, as we did for our Miss Lady Alex Cookies, following steps 1–4 on page 18.

2 Mix up your royal icing according to the packet instructions, then mix in 1 teaspoon of red extra paste. This is a seriously concentrated red food colouring and you should find that your royal icing quickly deepens to a shade of red. You can always add more colour if you are not happy with the depth of colour, but remember that the icing will dry into a darker shade.

3 Fill your piping bag one-quarter full. Close up the open end of your piping bag and ensure that the icing is all squeezed down towards the piping nozzle/tip. Your piping bag should be closed so tightly that you only have to squeeze very gently to make the icing come out of the nozzle/tip.

4 To pipe ruffles, you will need to hold your piping bag at a 45° angle, with the leaf piping nozzle/tip laid so that it is horizontal, and squeeze gently until the icing starts to touch the cookie. The key is to create folds of icing by piping a small amount and then moving the piping bag back slightly (still piping as you go) so that you pipe again over the last little bit. By rocking your piping bag from left to right, in a figure-of-eight motion, around the cookie, you will create a ruffle effect. You may find this easiest if you turn the cookie in one hand and rock your piping bag in the other. Repeat to decorate all of the cookies, refilling the piping bag as necessary. Leave the icing to dry.

Miss Tempest Rose Cupcakes

500 g / 1 lb. 2 oz. white
   sugarpaste

teal food colouring paste

12 Cupcakes (see page 9)

½ quantity Buttercream
   (see page 13)

cornflour / cornstarch,
   for dusting

FOR THE ROSES:

150 g / 5½ oz. pre-coloured
   ruby red sugarpaste

hologram red edible glitter

EQUIPMENT:

marzipan spacers

a round cookie cutter the
   same size as the top of
   your cupcake

a plastic document wallet

Makes 12

It's time to rock 'n' rose with your very own handmade sugar roses! Practice makes perfect and these cupcakes, inspired by the dazzling Tempest Rose, are pure perfection.

1 Following steps 1–3 on page 22, begin by dyeing your sugarpaste teal and using it to cover your buttercream-coated cupcakes, as we did for our Miss Anna Fur Laxis Cupcakes.

2 For the roses, knead your red sugarpaste to warm it through before rolling it into a sausage shape around 15 mm/¾ inch thick.

3 Cut 10 small discs of between 3–5 mm/⅛–¼ inch thick from this sugarpaste and place them inside a plastic document wallet (we use these because they are non-stick). Press down on each disc to flatten slightly and run your finger along the top edge of each disc to thin it out even more. This thin top edge will be the top of each petal.

4 Remove the smallest disc from the wallet and roll it into a tight coil by tucking in the left edge and rolling the disc in-between your thumb and index finger. This is the centre of your rose.

5 Lay your next petal around the centre of your rose, placing it slightly higher than the centre and wrapping the bottom around tightly. Your next petal sits directly opposite this one, completing your second layer of petals.

6 Your third layer of petals should be made of three more petals, each laid on and wrapped around as in step 5. Add a fourth layer of petals in the same way, using up your remaining four petals to complete the rose.

7 Cut away the excess from the bottom of your rose with a sharp knife and discard. Sprinkle your rose with a little red edible glitter and fix to the top of your cupcake with a tiny dab of water. Repeat for the remaining cupcakes.

Miss Bettie Mae Mini Cakes

750 g / 1 lb. 10 oz. white sugarpaste

yellow food colouring paste

16 x 5-cm / 2-inch Mini Cakes (see page 9)

1 quantity Buttercream (see page 13)

cornflour / cornstarch, for dusting

blossom tint dust colours in brown and terracotta

clear alcohol (I recommend vodka!)

16 sugarpaste roses (see page 28)

EQUIPMENT:

16 x 16-cm / 6½-inch lengths of thin red ribbon

an artist's palette for mixing your colours

a paintbrush

(see also equipment required for covering a cake on page 14)

Makes 16

Fierce and fabulous, wrapped in leopard print, these mini cakes are a homage to an icon – the Queen of Pin-ups, Bettie Mae Page.

1 Begin by dyeing your sugarpaste yellow. Cover your mini cakes in buttercream and then the sugarpaste, using the same technique as we used in The Art of Covering Up on pages 14–15. Remember that mini cakes can be a little fiddly so take your time! Finish each cake with the red ribbon.

2 For your leopard print, you will need to make edible paint using the dust colours. Sprinkle a small amount of dust colour into an artist's palette and mix with a few drops of clear alcohol to make a paste. You can purchase a special cake decorating alcohol for this job but I find that vodka is far more economical and works in the same way – we use alcohol because it evaporates faster than water.

3 To create your leopard print pattern, start by painting sporadic blotches of colour using the terracotta food paint. Wiggle your brush as you paint to add to the organic feel of the pattern.

4 Using your brown paint, wiggle your brush around each of your terracotta blotches to create a darker border around each one. Try to be as random as you can and maybe even leave some borders unfinished. Dab some little darker spots here and there between the larger spots.

5 I think that these cakes look great crowned with a single glittery rose. Follow the ingredients and instructions detailed in steps 2–7 of the Miss Tempest Rose Cupcakes on page 28, affixing a rose to the top of each mini cake with a tiny dab of water.

Coquettish Cookies

500 g / 1 lb. 2 oz. white
   sugarpaste

creamy peach food colouring
   paste

12 Classic Cookies
   (see page 12)

cornflour / cornstarch,
   for dusting

250 g / 2 cups royal icing
   sugar

pearlescent white metallic
   food paint

EQUIPMENT:

marzipan spacers

the same cookie cutter you
   used to make the cookies

a small heart-shaped cookie
   cutter

a parchment piping bag
   fitted with a leaf
   nozzle/tip

a parchment piping bag
   fitted with a fine round
   nozzle/tip

a paintbrush

Makes 12

Inspired by the incredible teasewear creations of the
ladies at Holloway Smith Noir. You could even use
a little royal icing to attach these to your…

1 Dye your sugarpaste with creamy peach paste, adding it a little at a time
   with a cocktail stick/toothpick. Once the colour is evenly kneaded in,
remove one-quarter of the sugarpaste and set aside. Add more paste to the
remaining three-quarters of the sugarpaste to achieve a deeper shade of peach.
Roll it out and use it to cover your cookies, as we did for our Miss Lady Alex
Cookies, following steps 1–4 on page 18. Using the heart-shaped cookie cutter,
cut out the centre of the sugarpaste on your cookie.

2 Knead and roll out your lighter shade of sugarpaste, again using the marzipan
   spacers – it is important that this centrepiece is the same thickness as the rest
of the sugarpaste covering. Cut out a heart using the same cookie cutter, paint a little
water onto its back, and use this heart to fill the centre of your cookie.

3 Roll out a small amount of your leftover dark sugarpaste to a thickness of
   2–3 mm / 1⁄16–1⁄8 inch. Cut out three 3-cm / 1¼-inch strips, about 8 mm / 3⁄8 inch
wide, and cut one of these strips in half to make up the tails of your bow. Arrange
them on top of your cookie, securing using a tiny dab of water.

4 Take your two longer strips and fold each one in half to create the loops of
   your bow. You will find that these look more animated if you flip each loop
onto its side. Pinch the open ends of these loops to make two teardrop shapes and
add these to your ribbon tails on the cookie to form your bow. Secure with a dab
of water. Finish your bow by covering the joins in the middle using another thin
strip of sugarpaste. You will need to cut this to a size that fits your bow.

5 Make up the royal icing according to the packet instructions and add a
   couple of drops of the creamy peach colour. Fill your piping bag fitted with
a leaf nozzle/tip one-quarter full and pipe a ruffle trim using the same method
that we used for our Miss Scarlet Delights Cookies on page 27.

6 Fill the piping bag fitted with the round nozzle/tip one-quarter full with royal
   icing and pipe two small pearls below the bow. Allow these to dry for at least
10 minutes before using the paintbrush to paint them with the pearlescent paint.

Miss Indigo Blue Mini Cakes

750 g / 1 lb. 10 oz. white
    sugarpaste

royal blue food colouring
    paste

16 x 5-cm / 2-inch Mini
    Cakes (see page 9)

1 quantity Buttercream
    (see page 13)

cornflour / cornstarch,
    for dusting

a selection of sugar diamonds
    and dragées

EQUIPMENT:

16 x 16-cm / 6½-inch
    lengths of thin blue ribbon

(see also equipment required
    for covering a cake on
    page 14)

Makes 16

Sparkling and stunning, like the sky at night, these mini
cakes are a decadent treat to enliven Afternoon Tea!
Inspired by the twirly girl, Miss Indigo Blue.

1 Begin by dyeing your sugarpaste royal blue. Cover your mini-cakes in
buttercream and then the sugarpaste, using the same technique as we
used in The Art of Covering Up on pages 14–15. You may find this a little
fiddly at first as smaller cakes require more nimble fingers than larger ones!
Finish each cake with the blue ribbon.

2 Take a selection of your larger sugar diamond and dragées and press each
one firmly into the sugarpaste on top of your mini cake. You will need to
do this just after you have covered your mini cakes, while the sugarpaste is still
soft. Be decisive with each diamond and dragée that you add and push them in
firmly. You are relying on the sugarpaste itself to hold each piece in place – if you
wiggle the pieces around as you add them, they will fall off!

3 Create a cascade of tiny edible jewels by continuing to add your smaller
pieces as if they were falling down the sides of your mini cakes. Add
fewer details as you work down the sides and stop just short of the bottom
of each mini cake.

Miss Fleur du Mal Cookies

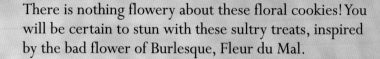

12 Classic Cookies
(see page 12)

500 g / 4 cups royal icing
sugar

spruce green food colouring
paste

cornflour / cornstarch,
for dusting

a selection of prepared Sugar
Flowers – about 3 per
cookie (see page 25 –
these can be made ahead
of time)

hologram red edible glitter

EQUIPMENT:

a parchment piping bag
fitted with a small piping
nozzle / tip

a plastic squeezy bottle

a cocktail stick / toothpick

Makes 12

There is nothing flowery about these floral cookies! You will be certain to stun with these sultry treats, inspired by the bad flower of Burlesque, Fleur du Mal.

1 To flood your cookies with royal icing and create that beautifully polished topping, you will need to prepare your royal icing in two halves. Make up your royal icing according to the packet instructions until the icing is stiff but not brittle – you need to get it to soft peaks. Tint the full batch of icing with spruce green food colouring paste, then spoon one half of this into the piping bag, close up the bag and set aside.

2 You will now need a thinner royal icing to flood the top of your cookie. Start by adding a teaspoon of cold water to your remaining icing. Mix through for a minute and remove your beaters. The icing is ready for flooding when you can remove your beaters, count to seven, and see no peaks or ripples in the bowl. Flooding icing should be like a deliciously thick liquid. If you are not there yet, add a little more water until you reach this stage. I recommend pouring your flooding icing into a squeezy bottle as it reduces the mess!

3 Use your stiffer royal icing in the piping bag to pipe a circular line around the edge of your cookie. Think of this as your floodgate – you want the line of icing to create a perfect circle with no gaps.

4 Flood your cookie by squeezing your flooding icing within the lines of your floodgate, leaving a gap of 2–3 mm / 1/16–1/8 inch. You will need to work quickly as this icing sets fast! Hold your cookie on a work surface and shake it from side to side. You should see the icing start to level out towards the edges. Keep shaking until the icing has joined up with the floodgate to cover the top of your cookie with no gaps. Any stubborn gaps can be filled by gently teasing the icing into the gap with a cocktail stick/toothpick. Leave your icing to dry overnight.

5 Once your icing is dry, you can arrange your sugar flowers on top of your cookie. My flowers have been made using ruby red sugarpaste and sprinkled with hologram red edible glitter. Secure each flower in place with a little of the stiff royal icing used as a glue. Finish the cookie off with a generous sprinkling of edible glitter.

Miss Sally Rand Cupcakes

500 g / 1 lb. 2 oz. white
  sugarpaste

grape food colouring paste

½ quantity Buttercream
  (see page 13)

12 Cupcakes (see page 9)

cornflour / cornstarch,
  for dusting

250 g / 2 cups royal icing
  sugar

dark gold metallic food paint

EQUIPMENT:

marzipan spacers

a round cookie cutter the
  same size as the top of
  your cupcake

a parchment piping bag
  fitted with a fine round
  nozzle / tip

a paintbrush

Makes 12

These cupcakes take their inspiration from Miss Sally
Rand's feather fan dance – an inspiration to so many…

1 Following steps 1–3 on page 22, begin by dyeing your sugarpaste grape
and using it to cover your buttercream-coated cupcakes, as we did for
our Miss Anna Fur Laxis Cupcakes.

2 Mix up your royal icing according to the packet instructions, and fill
your piping bag one-quarter full. Pipe a long line up the centre of your
cupcake, with a slight curve in it, to form the central feather of your fan.

3 While the royal icing is still wet, take a dampened paintbrush and use
this to smudge the lines of icing out. This should start to create a series
of very fine lines of icing, which fill up a fluffy feather shape. This technique
is called 'brush embroidery'. You will need to work on one line of icing at
a time, but a little time spent creates a truly stunning result.

4 Repeat this process, piping lines to create a fan-shaped arrangement of
feathers, all meeting in a point at the bottom edge. Finish your fan by
piping a series of curved lines around the feathers to create a scalloped edge
at the top of your fan, then brush this outwards, away from the feathers in the
same way.

5 Pipe a 'V' shape at the pointed edge of your fan. Allow the icing to dry for
10 minutes before painting with the gold food paint.

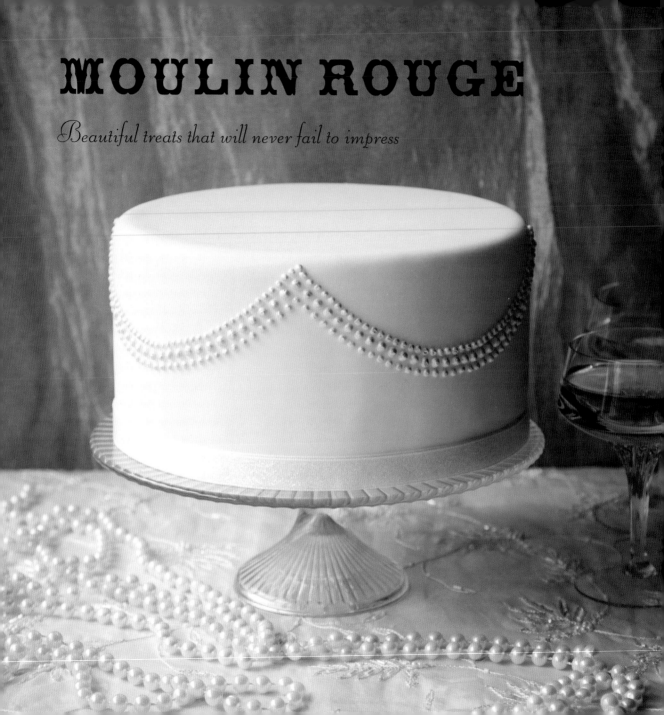

MOULIN ROUGE

Beautiful treats that will never fail to impress

Miss Banbury Cross Cake

a 20-cm/8-inch Cake in
   any flavour you wish
   (see pages 9–11)

1 quantity Buttercream
   (see page 13)

1 kg/2¼ lbs. white
   sugarpaste

cornflour/cornstarch,
   for dusting

125 g/1 cup royal icing
   sugar

pearlescent white metallic
   food paint

EQUIPMENT:

white ribbon

baking parchment

scissors

sticky tape

a cocktail stick/toothpick

a parchment piping bag
   fitted with a fine round
   nozzle/tip

a parchment piping bag
   fitted with a medium
   round nozzle/tip

a paintbrush

(see also equipment required
   for covering a cake on
   page 14)

Serves up to 20

The original 'Bulletproof Blonde', adorned with swags
of shimmering pearls.

1 Begin by covering your cake in buttercream and then sugarpaste, using the
same technique as we used in The Art of Covering Up on pages 14–15,
finishing with the white ribbon.

2 To create your swag pattern, you will need to create a collar for your cake
using baking parchment. A covered 20-cm/8-inch cake has a circumference
of approximately 63 cm/25 inches, so you will need to cut your paper to this
length and to the height of your cake, which will typically be 8–10 cm/3–4
inches. Fold this collar in half and then in half again to create four equal sections.
With your paper collar still folded, cut a semi-circle out of the top edge of the
collar, running from edge to edge. If you would like to be precise about this, you
can draw around a cup or a plate to achieve a perfect semi-circle.

3 Open out your paper collar and wrap it around the sides of your cake,
securing with a little sticky tape. Your cut-away semi-circles should have
created a swag pattern along the top edge of the collar. Using a cocktail stick/
toothpick, scratch a faint line into the sugarpaste along the swag line. Once you
have scratched the outline all the way around your cake, remove the paper collar.

4 Mix up your royal icing according to the packet instructions and fill both
piping bags one-quarter full with the icing. Beginning with the piping bag
with the fine nozzle/tip, pipe a line of pearls all around your cake following your
swag guideline. To do this, hold your piping bag at a right-angle to the cake, very
nearly touching the surface, and squeeze the bag gently until you are happy with
the size of pearl that you have made. Stop piping and pull the nozzle/tip away. If
you get a small peak on your pearl, dampen this down with a paintbrush.

5 Use your piping bag fitted with the medium nozzle/tip to pipe a line
of larger pearls directly underneath the swag of smaller pearls.
Repeat this process once more with the smaller nozzle/tip so that you
have a triple strand of pearls.

6 Leave your pearls to dry for around an hour before painting
them with pearlescent white metallic food paint to
bring them to life.

Miss Kitten Von Mew Mini Cakes

750 g / 1 lb. 10 oz. white
    sugarpaste

creamy peach food colouring
    paste

16 x 5-cm / 2-inch Mini
    Cakes (see page 9)

½ quantity Buttercream
    (see page 13)

cornflour / cornstarch,
    for dusting

250 g / 2 cups royal icing
    sugar

EQUIPMENT:

16 x 16-cm / 6¼-inch lengths
    of thin peach ribbon

baking parchment

scissors

sticky tape

cocktail stick / toothpick or
    scribe tool

a parchment piping bag fitted
    with a leaf nozzle / tip

(see also equipment required
    for covering a cake on
    page 14)

Makes 16

This delicious purring pin-up is as pretty as a picture in peach.

1 Begin by dyeing your sugarpaste a nude shade using creamy peach food colouring paste. Cover your mini cakes in Buttercream and then the sugarpaste, using the same technique as we used in The Art of Covering Up on pages 14–15. Try not to rush these as smaller cakes require a little extra time to get your fingers around the sugarpaste. Finish each cake with the peach ribbon.

2 To create your swag pattern, make a small parchment collar to wrap around your mini cake. This will only need to be approximately 17 cm / 6¼ inches long and as tall as your mini cake. Fold this collar in half and – while still folded – cut a semi-circle from the top. Wrap the collar around your mini cake and secure with sticky tape.

3 Use your cocktail stick / toothpick to mark a line around the top of the collar to create the swag pattern around your mini cake. Remove the parchment collar. You will be able to use this same collar on as many mini cakes as you like so do not throw it away.

4 Mix up your royal icing according to the packet instructions and tint it a slightly lighter shade of peach to the sugarpaste using the food colouring paste. Fill the piping bag one-quarter full with the icing.

5 Pipe a ruffle trim along the guideline that you have marked. A ruffle trim is created by piping in a back and forth motion using a leaf piping nozzle so that the line of icing is folded over itself. This technique, also used for our Miss Scarlet Delights Cookies, is explained in more detail in step 4 on page 27. To pipe ruffles onto the side of mini cakes, you may find it more comfortable to gently hold your cake and tilt it away from you. This will give you a flatter surface to pipe onto.

6 Allow your ruffle swags to dry for at least 10 minutes before piping a second ruffle swag directly above your first one to create a double ruffle.

Miss Eliza Delite Cupcakes

500 g / 1 lb. 2 oz. white
    sugarpaste

sky blue food colouring paste

½ quantity Buttercream
    (see page 13)

12 Cupcakes (see page 9)

125 g / 1 cup royal icing
    sugar

cornflour / cornstarch,
    for dusting

dark and light silver metallic
    food paints (or silver
    lustre dusts)

EQUIPMENT:

marzipan spacers

a round cookie cutter the
    same size as the top of
    your cupcake

a parchment piping bag
    fitted with a fine round
    nozzle / tip

a paintbrush

Makes 16

Dressed in sky blue and sparkling silvers, this glittering star just stepped out of a dream.

1 Following steps 1–3 on page 22, begin by dyeing your sugarpaste sky blue and using it to cover your buttercream-coated cupcakes, as we did for our Miss Anna Fur Laxis Cupcakes on page 22.

2 Mix up your royal icing according to the packet instructions, and fill your piping bag one-quarter full. Pipe a line of pearls down the centre of your cupcake by squeezing very gently on your piping bag until you are happy with the size of your pearl. Dampen down any pointy edges with the paintbrush.

3 Pipe a second line of pearls across the centre of your cupcake – creating a cross pattern – and then pipe another two lines of pearls on the diagonal.

4 We are now going to use our piping bag to turn four of our lines of pearls into leaf shapes. Pipe a curved line of pearls from the centre of the cupcake to the end of each line, ensuring that you widen your line in the middle of each section, tapering to a point at the edge of the cupcake. You should end up with something that looks like an elongated blossom shape.

5 Fill in any gaps within each long leaf shape area with more piped pearls, then allow the icing pearls to dry for at least 30 minutes.

6 Using the food paints, paint the pearls outlining the leaf dark silver and all of the other pearls light silver.

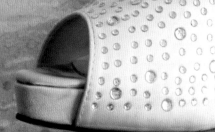

Holloway Smith Noir Cookies

500 g / 4 cups royal icing
    sugar

creamy peach food colouring
    paste

12 Classic Cookies
    (see page 12) made with
    a heart-shaped cutter

gold lustre dust

FOR THE FLOWERS:

125g / 1 cup royal icing sugar

½ teaspoon liquorice black
    food colouring paste

pearlescent white metallic
    food paint

dark gold metallic food paint

EQUIPMENT:

a large wide paintbrush

an artist's mixing palette

2 parchment piping bags
    fitted with fine round
    piping nozzles / tips

a fine round paintbrush

a parchment piping bag
    fitted with a small leaf
    piping nozzle / tip

Makes 12

Feel good about being naughty with these beautiful treats.

1 Begin making up 250 g / 2 cups of your royal icing and tint it with creamy peach colouring paste. Flood your cookies in the same way as we did for our Miss Fleur du Mal Cookies, following steps 1–4 on page 36.

2 Allow your icing to set for at least an hour before brushing with a gold lustre dust to make it shimmer and shine. The best way to go about this is to shake a small amount of the lustre dust into your artist's palette and brush it onto your cookie using a large, wide paintbrush.

3 Prepare the rest of your royal icing according to the packet instructions and spoon a little of it into one of the piping bags fitted with the fine round nozzle / tip and set aside. Throw a generous dollop of liquorice black food colouring paste into the remaining icing and continue to mix until you are happy with the consistency. You need the icing to hold a soft peak. Now fill the other piping bag with the fine nozzle / tip one-quarter full with the black icing.

4 Pipe 3 or 4 small flower outlines onto one corner of your cookie. While the royal icing is still wet, dampen the fine round paintbrush and use this to smudge the lines of icing towards the centre of each flower. Finish each flower with a dot piped into its centre and pipe a border around this corner area in black royal icing.

5 Pipe a line of 3 black pearls down the centre of your cookie, leaving enough space between them to allow for white pearls.

6 Using the piping bag with the white icing, pipe two small white pearls between your black pearls and one large pearl underneath. Allow these white pearls to dry for at least 10 minutes before painting the small pearls with pearlescent white food paint, and the large pearl with dark gold.

7 Fill the empty piping bag with the leaf nozzle / tip one-quarter full with more black icing and, following step 4 on page 27, finish each cookie with a ruffle trim in the same way as we did for our Miss Scarlet Delights Cookies. Repeat to decorate all of the cookies and leave the icing to dry.

Miss Missy Malone Cupcakes

500 g / 1 lb. 2 oz. white
   sugarpaste

lemon yellow food colouring paste

½ quantity Buttercream
   (see page 13)

12 Cupcakes (see page 9)

cornflour / cornstarch,
   for dusting

125 g / 1 cup royal icing sugar

gold dragées

FOR THE FLOWERS:

1 teaspoon tylose powder

250 g / 9 oz. white sugarpaste

EQUIPMENT:

a round cookie cutter the same
   size as the top of your
   cupcake

a paintbrush

a small non-stick rolling pin

a large rose petal cutter

a parchment piping bag fitted
   with a medium round
   nozzle / tip

Makes 12

Cupcakes camouflaged in petals for a Rockabilly Bombshell.

1 Following steps 1–3 on page 22, begin by dyeing the 500 g / 1 lb. 2 oz. sugarpaste yellow and using it to cover your buttercream-coated cupcakes, as we did for our Miss Anna Fur Laxis Cupcakes on page 22. Be extra careful to keep any leftover sugarpaste wrapped tightly in a plastic bag as we will use this later.

2 For the flowers, knead the tylose powder into the 250 g / 9 oz. sugarpaste until it is completely incorporated. Divide this paste into 3 pieces – one smaller, one medium-sized and one larger – and then colour each piece to a different intensity. I have used 1 drop of yellow colouring for the smaller piece, 2 drops for the medium-sized piece, and 3 drops for the largest piece.

3 Roll out the darkest shade of paste to around 2 mm / 1⁄16 inch thick (you may need to dust your work surface and rolling pin with cornflour / cornstarch) and cut out 60 petals using the rose petal cutter. Allow these petals to dry on an uneven surface – try crumpling a sheet of baking parchment and laying the petals over the bumps – for at least 4 hours. Repeat with the remaining sugarpaste, cutting out 48 petals in the medium shade of yellow, and 36 in the lightest shade.

4 Using your leftover sugarpaste from covering your cupcakes, roll 12 marble-sized balls and attach one to the centre of each cupcake with a dab of water.

5 For each cupcake, paint a ring of water around your central ball and lay 5 of your darkest petals around the ball, so that they rest on the surface of the cake. Your petals will have one pointed end, which should be gently pushed into the ball.

6 Lightly paint the exposed area of the central ball with water and arrange 4 of your medium-coloured petals around the ball so that they rest on top of the petals below them, gently pushing the pointed ends into the central ball.

7 Arrange your lightest petals in a circle on top of your previous layer of petals. You may find that you have completely covered the central ball. If you still have some of the ball exposed, push the pointed ends of your petals into it as before.

8 To finish the cakes, prepare the royal icing according to the packet instructions and fill the piping bag one-quarter full. Pipe a little royal icing into the middle of your top layer of petals and drop gold dragées onto this sticky surface; cluster them to create the centre of a flower and then leave the icing to dry.

Miss Rainbow Sparkles Mini Cakes

21 x 5-cm/2-inch Mini
Cakes (see page 9)

2 quantities Buttercream
(see page 13)

1.5 kg/3 lb. 3 oz. white
sugarpaste

250 g/2 cups royal icing
sugar

cornflour/cornstarch,
for dusting

FOR THE FLOWERS:

3 teaspoons tylose powder

700 g/1 lb. 9 oz. white
sugarpaste

food colouring pastes in red
extra, orange, yellow, mint
green, sky blue, royal blue
and violet

edible glaze spray

hologram white edible glitter

EQUIPMENT:

21 x 16-cm/6½-inch lengths
of thin ribbon (3 in each
colour of the rainbow)

a selection of flower cutters
and moulds (I have used
hydrangea, cherry
blossom and petunia)

(see also equipment required
for covering a cake on
page 14)

Makes 21

Taste the sweetness of a glittering rainbow! This project
requires a little forethought and pre-planning but is
incredibly simple and oh-so stunning when finished.
You will be glad of the little effort that you put in!

1 Begin by covering your mini cakes in buttercream and then white sugarpaste,
using the same technique detailed in The Art of Covering Up on pages
14–15. These can be a little tricky as they are small and awkward to get your
hands around – persevere with patience. Finish each cake with a ribbon.

2 To create your rainbow of flower-encrusted mini cakes, you will need to
prepare seven different colours of simple sugar flowers. (These can be made
days and weeks in advance so plan ahead and have your flowers stored safely in
cardboard boxes ready to be stuck to your cakes.) Knead the tylose powder into
the 700 g/1 lb. 9 oz. sugarpaste (this causes the sugarpaste to dry hard and hold
its shape), then divide it into 7 equal portions. Tint each portion a different colour
of the rainbow with the colouring pastes.

3 Following the method we used to create flowers for our Miss Strawberry
Siren Cake, steps 3–4 on page 25, make roughly 15–20 flowers for each
mini cake, though this will depend upon the size of flower that you are making.
I recommend making a few extra in case you have any bald spots! To cover your
entire display, you'll need around 60 flowers in each of your 7 colours.

4 Prepare your royal icing according to the packet instructions and have this
ready as your 'glue' to affix each flower to your mini cakes. Beginning at the
bottom of each mini cake, attach each flower by spreading a small amount of royal
icing onto its back and pressing it gently onto your mini cake. Always start at the
bottom of each cake so that the weight of the higher flowers is supported by the
lower flowers.

5 Allow your completed mini cakes to dry for at least 30 minutes before
spraying with an edible glaze and sprinkling with glitter. By doing this,
your flowers will look like they are straight out of the fantastical gardens of Oz!

6 Arrange your beautiful mini cakes on a tiered Perspex cake stand.

Café de Paris

Putting all of your new skills together to the delight of the crowd

Miss Catherine D'Lish Cake

1 kg / 2¼ lbs. white
   sugarpaste

creamy peach food colouring
   paste

a 20-cm / 8-inch Cake in
   any flavour you wish
   (see pages 9–11)

1 quantity Buttercream
   (see page 13)

cornflour / cornstarch,
   for dusting

250 g / 2 cups royal icing
   sugar

liquorice black food
   colouring paste

EQUIPMENT:

black lace ribbon

a parchment piping bag
   fitted with a fine round
   nozzle / tip

a fine paintbrush

(see also equipment required
   for covering a cake on
   page 14)

Serves up to 20

This timeless and elegant design is simply stunning in lace, dedicated to a virtuoso and true Burlesque star.

1 Begin by dyeing your sugarpaste a pale nude colour, using the creamy peach food colouring paste. Cover your cake in buttercream and then the sugarpaste, using the same technique as we used in The Art of Covering Up on pages 14–15, finishing with a black lace ribbon.

2 Prepare your royal icing according to the packet instructions, then tint it black with the liquorice black food colouring paste. To get your icing really dark, you will need to be bold and add a good ½ teaspoon of the paste, then continue to mix until you are happy with the consistency. Fill the piping bag one-quarter full with the black icing.

3 To create the lace effect on this cake, begin by piping a large flower shape, approximately 4-cm / 1½-inches diameter on the top of your cake. As soon as you have piped this shape, take a slighty dampened paintbrush and use it to drag the line that you have piped into the centre of the shape. You are aiming to turn your smooth, solid line into a line that is smooth on its outside edges and rough on its inside edges.

4 Once you have completed this large flower, take your piping bag and pipe another smaller flower shape inside the large one. Take your paintbrush and brush the lines of this flower in the same way as before. Repeat this process with one last tiny flower in the very centre and finish with a small black pearl piped into the middle.

5 The true impact of this lace effect will only become apparent once you have repeated this entire process with large flower shapes covering the cake. Any bald areas can be filled with tiny dots of black royal icing.

1 kg / 2¼ lbs. white
  sugarpaste

claret food colouring paste

a 20-cm / 8-inch cake in
  any flavour you wish
  (see pages 9–11)

1 quantity Buttercream
  (see page 13)

cornflour / cornstarch,
  for dusting

250 g / 2 cups royal icing
  sugar

FOR THE FLOWER:

1 teaspoon tylose powder

250 g / 9 oz. white
  sugarpaste

hologram red edible glitter

EQUIPMENT:

a claret ribbon

baking parchment

scissors

sticky tape

a cocktail stick / toothpick

a parchment piping bag
  fitted with a fine round
  nozzle / tip

a paintbrush

a parchment piping bag fitted
  with a leaf nozzle / tip

a large rose petal cutter

(see also equipment required
  for covering a cake on
  page 14)

Serves up to 20

Miss Polly Rae Cake

Never was there a Polly so pretty.

1 Begin by dyeing your sugarpaste a pale claret. Cover your cake in buttercream and then the sugarpaste, using the same technique as we used on pages 14–15, finishing with a claret ribbon. Wrap any leftover sugarpaste in clingfilm / plastic wrap.

2 Following steps 2–3 on page 41, create a paper collar and mark an outline of swags around the cake, as we did for the Miss Banbury Cross Cake.

3 Mix up your royal icing according to the packet instructions and tint it a deep claret colour with the paste. Fill the piping bag fitted with the fine round nozzle / tip one-quarter full with the icing. Use this to pipe a line of pearls along the swag line that you have marked out. Remember to stop squeezing your piping bag when you are happy with the size of your pearl and pull the nozzle / tip gently away from the cake. If you are left with a peak, dampen it with a paintbrush.

4 Fill the piping bag fitted with the leaf nozzle / tip with more claret icing and use this to pipe a ruffle trim along the top edge of your cake, following the method for ruffles we used on the Miss Scarlet Delights Cookies in step 4 on page 27.

5 For the flower, knead the tylose powder into the 250 g / 9 oz. sugarpaste, then divide it into 3 pieces. Colour each piece to a different intensity of claret. Try to avoid having any one of these pieces in exactly the same shade as your cake.

6 Using the same method as we used for our Miss Missy Malone Cupcakes on page 49, follow step 3 to create petals for a giant flower to crown the top of your cake. You will need to make 9 dark petals for your bottom layer, 7 medium petals for your middle layer, and 3 light petals for your top layer.

7 Using your reserved sugarpaste, roll a ball approximately the size of a golf ball and cut the bottom edge away from it to create a flat surface. Stick this flat surface in the centre of your cake using a dab of water. Continuing with the method from page 49, follow steps 5–7 to continue building your flower.

8 Returning to your piping bag fitted with the fine round nozzle / top, finish off your giant flower by piping some pearls into the centre. Do not worry about dampening down any peaks on these pearls as the slightly rough texture looks great here. Finish the centre of the flower with a sprinkling of red glitter.

Miss Gypsy Rose Cupcakes

500 g / 1 lb. 2 oz. white
    sugarpaste

liquorice black food
    colouring paste

12 Cupcakes (see page 9)

½ quantity Buttercream
    (see page 13)

cornflour / cornstarch,
    for dusting

FOR THE ROSES:

300 g / 10½ oz. white
    sugarpaste

150 g / 5½ oz. pre-coloured
    black sugarpaste

hologram white edible glitter

EQUIPMENT:

marzipan spacers

a round cookie cutter the
    same size as the top of
    your cupcake

a plastic document wallet

Makes 12

A marvel in monochrome, completely covered by the spotlight, in tribute to a true original.

1 Begin by dyeing your 500 g / 1 lb. 2 oz. of sugarpaste a pale silver colour using a small amount of the black food colouring paste. Following steps 1–3 on page 22, cover your cupcakes with the buttercream and then the silver sugarpaste as we did for our Miss Anna Fur Laxis Cupcakes.

2 We are going to make 3 different coloured roses; 12 white, 12 grey and 12 black. To make your grey, you will need to add a little black colouring paste to 150 g / 5½ oz. of your white sugarpaste and knead in, adding a tiny bit at a time until you are happy with the shade.

3 To make a rose, knead the sugarpaste to warm it through before rolling it into a sausage shape around 15 mm / ¾ inch thick. Cut 6 small discs of between 3–5 mm / ⅛–¼ inch thick from this sugarpaste and place them inside a plastic document wallet. Press down on each disc to flatten slightly and run your finger along the top edge of each disc to thin out even more. This thin top edge will be the top of each petal.

4 Remove the smallest disc from the wallet and roll it into a tight coil by tucking in the left edge and rolling the disc in-between your thumb and index finger. This is the centre of your rose.

5 Lay your next petal around the centre of your rose, placing it slightly higher than the centre and wrapping the bottom around tightly. Your next petal sits directly opposite this one, completing your second layer of petals.

6 Your third layer should be made of 3 more petals, each wrapped around as before. Squeeze the bottom of your rose gently to ensure that the petals are secure, then cut away the excess from the bottom of your rose with a sharp knife. Sprinkle your roses with edible glitter to make them glisten.

7 Repeat steps 4–6 until you have made 3 roses for each cupcake, one in each shade. Assemble the roses on top of your cupcake in a little cluster, affixing each one with a dab of water.

Miss Immodesty Blaize Cake

a 20-cm/8-inch Cake in
 any flavour you wish
 (see pages 9–11)

1 quantity Buttercream
 (see page 13)

1 kg/2¼ lbs. pre-coloured
 ruby red sugarpaste

cornflour/cornstarch,
 for dusting

500 g/4 cups royal icing
 sugar

liquorice black and red extra
 food colouring paste

silver dragées

red metallic food paint

EQUIPMENT:

black sequinned ribbon

2 parchment piping bags
 fitted with fine round
 nozzles/tips

a parchment piping bag
 fitted with a medium
 round nozzle/tip

a paintbrush

(see also equipment required
 for covering a cake on
 page 14)

Serves up to 20

The tiger-eyed temptress in rubies.

1 Begin by covering your cake in buttercream and then in sugarpaste as we did in The Art of Covering Up on pages 14–15. I have used a sugarpaste that has been pre-coloured – please do not attempt to achieve this depth of red by adding colour to white sugarpaste as you will get in a very sticky mess before you reach this shade. Finish the cake with a black sequinned ribbon.

2 Prepare your royal icing according to the packet instructions. Spoon roughly one-third of the icing into another bowl and tint it black. Tint the remaining two-thirds of the icing with red extra. Fill one of the piping bags with a fine nozzle/tip with liquorice black icing so it is one-quarter full, and the remaining two piping bags with the red icing in the same way.

3 Begin by piping one large red pearl onto the centre of the top of your cake using the piping bag with the medium nozzle/tip. Dampen down any point on the pearl with a paintbrush to create a lovely rounded pearl. Leave this to dry for at least 10 minutes to avoid damaging it while you add more details to the design.

4 Pipe a thin line of black royal icing around your large red pearl and use this as an adhesive for a ring of silver dragées around your pearl.

5 Using your fine-tipped red piping bag, pipe 9 smaller red pearls around your central large red pearl. Remember to dampen down any peaks with your paintbrush as you go. Allow these to dry for at least 10 minutes before moving on.

6 Pipe a series of thin lines around these nine smaller pearls using your black royal icing. Press silver dragées into these lines so that they surround each of your smaller red pearls, and you are left with a brooch-style decoration.

7 Repeat this process to create a series of these red pearl and dragée brooches around the sides of your cake. Aim to produce at least another 4–6 brooches.

8 Fill in the gaps between your brooches with a series of scattered piped red and black pearls. Use all of your piping bags to vary their sizes and colours.

9 Allow your pearls to dry for at least 30 minutes before painting all of your red pearls with red metallic food paint to make them shiny. The resulting effect will be a scattering of both shining red jewels and black pearls.

Miss Vicky Butterfly Mini Cakes

16 x 5-cm/2-inch Mini Cakes (see page 9)

1 quantity Buttercream (see page 13)

750 g/1 lb. 10 oz. pre-coloured bottle-green sugarpaste

cornflour/cornstarch, for dusting

500 g/4 cups royal icing sugar

teal food colouring paste

light brown food colouring paste

mint green food colouring paste

liquorice black food colouring paste

EQUIPMENT:

16 x 16-cm/6½-inch lengths of thin black ribbon

a parchment piping bag fitted with a medium round nozzle/tip

2 parchment piping bags fitted with fine round nozzles/tips

a cocktail stick/toothpick

a paintbrush

a Perspex cake stand, optional

(see also equipment required for covering a cake on page 14)

Makes 16

Graceful and elegant peacock nocturne.

1 Begin by covering your mini cakes in buttercream and then sugarpaste, using the same technique as we used in The Art of Covering Up on pages 14–15, finishing each cake with the black ribbon. Set aside a little time for this task as covering small cakes requires patience.

2 Prepare your royal icing according to the packet instructions and divide it between 3 bowls. Tint the first bowl teal, the second bowl light brown and the final bowl mint green using the colouring pastes. Fill the piping bag fitted with the medium nozzle/tip one-quarter full with the teal icing, and the fine nozzle/tipped bags one-quarter full with each of the other colours.

3 Using the teal icing, pipe a large pearl, 1-cm/½-inch in diameter, halfway up one side of each of your mini cakes. This pearl will form the central 'eye' of the peacock feathers. Allow 10 minutes for the icing to dry.

4 Using the piping bag filled with light brown icing and holding your nozzle just away from the surface of your mini cake, pipe a ring of icing around the teal central eye. While this icing is still wet, take a damp paintbrush and pull down lightly on the bottom edge of this ring to create a teardrop shape. Repeat for each mini cake and, again, allow 10 minutes for the icing to dry.

5 On each mini cake, using the mint green icing, pipe a ring around the brown border of the central eye. Use a cocktail stick/toothpick to feather the bottom edge of this ring by dragging the edge down, leaving it jagged.

6 Pipe 6 lines of mint green royal icing from the top of each mini cake to the ribbons, working each line around the eye. You should create a pointed teardrop shape. While the icing is still wet, use your damp paintbrush to feather these lines of icing.

7 To complete our feathers, use a damp paintbrush dipped into a little black colouring paste to paint the eye detail into the teal centre of each of your feathers. The shape that you are aiming for is much like a rounded heart shape.

8 Allow your mini cakes at least 30 minutes to dry before arranging them on a tiered Perspex cake stand. With each peacock feather pointing outwards, you should create the illusion of a large peacock tail.

Miss Dita Von Teese Cake

1 kg / 2¼ lbs. white
   sugarpaste

turquoise food colouring
   paste

a 20-cm / 8-inch Cake in
   any flavour you wish
   (see pages 9–11)

1 quantity Buttercream
   (see page 13)

cornflour / cornstarch,
   for dusting

500 g / 4 cups royal icing
   sugar

teal, creamy peach and hot
   pink food colouring pastes

silver dragées

EQUIPMENT:

pink sequinned ribbon

a cocktail stick / toothpick

3 parchment piping bags
   fitted with fine round
   nozzles / tips

a paintbrush

(see also equipment required
   for covering a cake on
   page 14)

Serves up to 20

Designed for a powder puff pin-up, this cake is an
intricate advocate of glamour at all times and in all things.

1 Begin by dyeing your sugarpaste a light blue shade with the turquoise food
colouring paste. Cover your cake in buttercream and then the sugarpaste,
using the same technique as we used in The Art of Covering Up on pages 14–15,
finishing with a pink sequinned ribbon.

2 Use a cocktail stick / toothpick to score some swirling lines all over your
cake. Think about having swirls coming out of other swirls and
interconnecting all around the sides and over the top of your cake.

3 Prepare your royal icing according to the packet instructions and divide it
between 3 bowls. With the food colouring pastes, tint the first bowl teal, the
second bowl peach and the final bowl hot pink. Fill each of the piping bags one-
quarter full with one of the coloured icings.

4 Choose a swirl line and pipe a line of dots in the teal-coloured royal icing.
Dampen down any points on the pearls with a paintbrush and continue
piping dots until your swirl comes to a natural end.

5 Select a second swirl line and pipe a line of dots with your peach-coloured
royal icing, again dampening down any points.

6 Select a third swirl line and pipe a line of dots with your hot pink-coloured
royal icing, again dampening down any points.

7 Continue piping dots along the lines, changing between the three icing
colours, until the cake is covered, so that you are left with swirls that are
connected but in different colours (I am not going to lie, this design takes some
time to complete. You may find that you are piping this cake for a couple of hours,
but the finished article is very much worth your hard work.) Fill any conspicuous
gaps in your decoration with silver dragées and leave the icing to dry.

Index